All Things New

All Things New

By Alma Garrett

authorHOUSE®

AuthorHouse™
1663 Liberty Drive
Bloomington, IN 47403
www.authorhouse.com
Phone: 1-800-839-8640

First published by AuthorHouse   08/01/2011

ISBN: 978-1-4634-4029-9 (sc)
ISBN: 978-1-4634-4030-5 (hc)
ISBN: 978-1-4634-4064-0 (ebk)

Library of Congress Control Number: 2011913196

Printed in the United States of America

This book is printed on acid-free paper.

Acknowledgment

Barbara Ann Gaines
9/19/40-1/7/2011

I can see Jesus carrying you over the threshold of eternity. I can see Him lifting the veil from your eyes and you seeing who you really are for the very first time; His princess, His bride. And He, the lover of your soul, your God and your eternal husband is well pleased with whom He sees. I see you dancing and clapping your hands. I see you rejoicing exceedingly glad. I hear you singing and shouting glory to His name. I feel your peace. I love you Mommy. Thank you for giving me Jesus.

Alma Garrett

Contents

2 Corinthians 5:17

Therefore, if anyone is in Christ, he is a new creation; old things have passed away; behold, all things have become new.

The Prodigal

I'm so glad to be back home.
I remember when I left my daddy's house
I wanted to live life on my own.
I didn't want to follow my Father's rules,
I didn't want to listen to wisdom
Like my mother taught me to.

I thought the grass was greener on the other side,
I wasted many years learning that was a lie.

I went out into the world
And started acting like a fool,
I got into a whole lot of trouble too.
I was always on the outside looking in,
Trying to fit in where I could get in,
Trying to fit in where I didn't belong.
I made a lot of bad choices
And I did a lot of wrong.

Before I knew it I was headed
Down the wrong track,
Before I knew it I lost my way back.

I was down on my luck and
I couldn't get up. I was stuck.
Stuck in a world of darkness where
Friendships proved to be untrue.
Where nothing got better,
No matter what I'd do,
Where delusions kept me
Blind to the truth

You see, I placed my life in the hands of death,
In the hands of the one who wishes my demise,
That ole serpent: "The Father of Lies".

The enemy of my soul was now in control.
I was lost, I was blind, and I could not see
All the traps he had laid out for me.

A slave to his biding, a slave to his will
I was chasing broken promises
And living for cheap thrills.

My innocence gone; A woman scorn
I was scared, I was lonely,
I was shamed and confused.
I didn't know what to do.

Then winds of grace blew my way
And I began to pray.
"LORD, I've made a mess of my life.
Will You forgive me? Will You make it right?

I haven't been much of a daughter,
I've offended my brothers and sisters,
I've sinned against my father,
I've broken my mother's heart:
And I don't know where to start.

I don't deserve forgiveness.
But I just want them to know,
That I'm sorry from the bottom of my soul:
Will you help me find my way back home,
So that I can tell them that I was wrong.

It's been a long journey,
I can't wait to get back home.

A long journey,
I'd been away far too long

I can't wait to see His face,
Ask His forgiveness and His grace

I can't wait;
I can't wait to get back home

I can't wait to get back home
To the presences of His charm

I can't wait to get back home
To the comfort of His warmth

Into the safety of His arms
That place where I belong

I can't wait to hear him say
"My child is FOUND today

The CROSS has made away
For LOVE she's here to stay

I can't wait;
I can't wait to get back home

As I made my way toward
My Father's house
I could see him from afar off.
He was standing, waiting, praying
That I would be found
And no longer lost.

He saw me coming,
He ran to meet me.
He fell on my neck,
He hugged and he kissed me.

His anger didn't burn against me,
He CELEBRATED my return
He REJOICED because he LOVES
And really missed me;

NO He didn't accuse me of
All I had done wrong'
He just welcomed me back
With OPENED ARMS.

And I'm so glad to be back home.

The Winds Of Grace

The winds of grace blew my way
And swept me off my feet
Saved my soul and made me whole
Redeeming love so dear so sweet!

My spirit leaped inside of me
When I heard him calling me
Most humbly my heart agreed
"Surrender all to God thy King
That He may reign in thee"

Then heaven's Son
Shinning bright and deep
Lifted me from sins deceit
With rays of light renewing me
Infusing holy life in me!

And all the angels celebrated
With lifted voice they did rejoice
For this child of the light
That was rescued from the night.

No longer blind, no longer lost
For Thy hand of mercy
Led me to the cross

To see how justice and mercy met
To forgive and set me free
To pay a debt I could not pay
With amazing love that pardon me.

Tis' JESUS!
The lover of my soul
God's chosen sacrifice
Who laid down His life

Who shed his precious blood,
Who paid the highest price
To make me his bride
To take me as his wife

Now captivated by His mercy
Smitten by my Beloved
I pledge myself to Thee
NOW, and through
All ETERNITY

I'll Always Praise And Thank You

I'll always praise and thank You
For coming to my rescue;
For laying down Your life for me
That day You hung on Calvary's tree;
For washing me in Your redeeming blood,
For filling me with gifts from above,
For keeping me in Your precious love

I'll always praise and thank You
For coming to my rescue;
For taking me out of the miry clay
For delivering me from
My wayward ways
For forgiving me for my sins each day
For keeping me from evil's sway
And not letting death have its way

I'll always praise and thank You
For coming to my rescue;
For striving along side of me,
For giving me the victory,
For not handing me over to my enemies
For opening my eyes so that I can see
That it's You who love me
Unconditionally

I'll always praise and thank You
For coming to my rescue
For standing me on the ROCK
The ROCK of SALVATION
A sure FOUNDATION

For breathing new life into me
And leading me to
Clear water streams
Where pastures are lush
And ever green

I'll always praise and thank You
For coming to my rescue

I was blind
But now I see
Thank You LORD
For rescuing me!

How Great And Awesome You Are!

For who in the skies can compare with the LORD!
He is more awesome than all that surround Him.

Psalm 89:6-7

LORD, when I think about
How great and awesome You are,
I think about Your Eternal Power
And Divine Nature, and how You're the
Self-Existing, Self-Sustaining One,
The ALPHA and OMEGA,
The BEGINNING and the END.

I think about creation and
How You spoke everything into being.
You said, "LET IT BE" and it was:
The heavens and all its hosts,
The stars, the moon,
The sun, the planets,
Angels and cherubim,
And how at Your command,
They all obey Your plan

I think about the birds, the bees,
The flowers, the trees,
The earth beneath my feet
And the air I breathe,
Majestic mountains, roaring seas;
And how You made it all
I think about how You took some dirt,
Some soil from the earth
And fashioned man;
How Your breath gave us life,

And I say, "Yes indeed,
We are the works of Your hands,
Vessels to reflect Your image and glory,
Mouth full of praise, telling Your story

Stories of Your awesome power,
Like how You defeat Your own enemies
And place them under Your feet;
Like when You parted the Red Sea
To let Your people go free.
And how Pharaohs army
Drowned in that sea

I think about the Promised Seed
And the Virgin Birth
And why You came to earth.
And I know that only a Loving God
A loving Father would place Himself
Into the womb of a woman to
Fulfilling His own plan, to redeem man

I think about how great a love,
You lavish on me, Your grace,
Your compassion, Your mercy
And how You sent Your
Only Son to rescue me

And how You raised my JESUS,
My SAVIOR from the dead
And how You've kept
Every WORD You've said

I think about how Jesus
Conquered death just to set me free;
And I believe

I think about the multitude of SOULS
I want to present to You,
And about seeing You face to face,
Singing forever and ever
Of Your Amazing Grace

Yes, when I think about how
Great and awesome You are,
I think about Your Righteousness,
Your Holiness, Your Sovereignty,
And I agree with the saints of old-
Abraham, Isaac, Jacob and Moses-

There is none that come close,
To THE LORD OF HOST
None who can match
Your power and might
And like the Psalmist David
I too say:

Holy is Your Name.
I'll forever sing Your praise.

God Of Mercy

God of Mercy, God of Love
Eternally faithful and
Gracious to those You love
Laying down Your life
To set the sinner free
Restoring back to humanity
Glory and dignity
Forgiving transgression
Remembering no sins
Forgiving iniquities
Our Savior, our Friend
From darkness to light
You brought us out
Banishing our fears
Our shame and our doubts
You've raised us up
From the valley below
You've changed our life
With the TRUTH we now KNOW
You cause us to triumph
To triumph in love
You've given us the victory
You've covered us with love

Reign, Rein, Rain

From eternity past
To infinity,
You Reign LORD
Before all created things
Seen and unseen;
Celestial beings,
The universe,
The galaxies
All creatures
Great and small
You Reign, LORD,
Above them all
At Your command
The seasons come and go,
Springtime, Harvest,
Summertime, Winter snow
Above nature
Your will is done;
You quite the sea,
You still the storm.
You Reign LORD,
You rein me in.
Even in the valley,
Where indecision tries
To toss me to and fro,
You whisper to me,
Telling me
Which way to go
You light my path.
You order my steps.
You chart out the
Course, of my destiny;

Always guiding me,
Leading me into victory;
Abundantly blessing me
Setting me free
You rain down treasures
From heaven above;
Your grace, Your mercy,
Your peace, Your love.
You Reign, LORD,
In every high place
Where man bows his
Heart to foreign gods;
Where idols are made
Of wood, stone and clay;
Where philosophies
Of the world deceive
The human race
Where hypocrisy
Laced with pride,
Greed and lust
Tries to take
Your place,
You Reign, LORD.
For Your Sovereignty
Is the highest Authority!

Wonder Of All Wonders

Wonder of all wonders,
The virgin birth;
The miracle and mystery of
How God came to earth.

Announced by Angels,
Worshipped by kings;
Heaven sings of
This glorious scene

Love pure and Holy, undefiled,
Wrapped in a manger,
In the form of a child

This gift, God's Son,
Our hope is for everyone.

Emmanuel;
The Holy One of Israel,
He came to save us, to reconcile;
To show us the way back to the Father
That we too may become
His sons and daughters

God gave His best
When the WORD became flesh
Son of God, Son of man;
The Lion and the Lamb,
Fulfilled His own plan to redeem man

He poured out His life on Calvary,
So that we can be with Him eternally

What gift do we give to the King of kings?
What can we offer Elo-him;
The Creator of everything?

Give Him your heart
For His throne;
Invite Him in
To make it His home

Give Him your praise,
Your adoration,
A surrendered life
In dedication

Give Him the glory
That He deserves;
Give Him your best
Where ever you serve.

Sit with Him in His secret place;
Beholding His beauty, seeking His face

He'll take our pain and the tears we cry
And perform miracles and wonders
In our contrite and broken lives

Worship Him
In Spirit,
In Truth,
In Word,
In Deed;
Trust Him,
With these gifts
He'll be well pleased.

John 1:17

"Thank You Father for Your favor that has been granted to me permanently and without condition; grace, mercy, favor, blessing and gifts in abundance through my Lord Jesus that enables me to do all that I am called to do and receive according to You will for my life"

But Who Do You Say That I AM

(You are the Christ, the Son of the living God)

You are the 'Seed' of a woman
You're 'Bethlehem's Babe'
The 'Promise of the Father'
'The Lamb' that was slain;

You're 'Fire by Night'
And a 'Cloud by Day'
You are my 'Bright Morning Star'
You're the 'Only Way'

You are the 'Lily of the Valley'
You're my 'Rose of Sharon'
My doctor and my lawyer;
You're my 'Burdon Barrier'

You are the 'Good Shepherd'
Who's looking after me;
Who laid down His life,
So that I can be free.

You're 'JESUS,' 'The CHRIST'
My souls delight;
You are the 'Whisper in the wind'
That makes everything alright.

You are my destiny;
My goal and my dream,
I'm Yours forever throughout Eternity.

You are the 'Son of God';
Yes, the 'Son of man'
You are the 'Lion and the Lamb'
You're the 'Great I AM.'

You are 'Deity;' In humanity . . .'
Who came to earth,
Just to rescue us me.

You are a 'Prophet like Moses',
My 'Prince of Peace'
You are the 'Great Missionary'
With Beautiful Feet.

You are the 'Word of God'
Standing sure and strong;
You are the 'King of kings'
Sitting on His throne;

You are my
'Kinsman Redeemer'
My 'Mordecai.'

You're my 'Faithful Husband'
And I'm your "Bride"

You Are The Good Shepherd

You are the Good Shepherd:
The One who loves
And cares for me
Your time,
Your energy,
All Your ability;
You pour into me
That I may grow
And flourish and be the
Best You meant for me
Oh the joy that floods my soul,
Knowing that You are in control
You satisfy my thirst
With early morning dew;
You fill me with Your presence,
And mercy always new
Your Spirit ever
Guiding me,
Leading me,
In the way
Teaching me,
Training me
In all I do and say.
Oh how I love You
Father,
My Savior
And my King
Knowing that You
Love me makes
My heart shout And sing!

All I Long To Do

Dear Holy Spirit,
I've counted the cost
And nothing would be lost.

No worldly gain,
No fortune, nor fame,
Can compare to the
Truth I've found in You.

I bow my will, I surrender all
I say "Yes" to Your call
To take up my cross and
Follow Jesus Is all I long to do.

Now help me keep my focus,
And not lose sight of You.

Keep me in Thy presence,
Let me know that You're near;

Fill me with Thy peace
Still my heart, quiet my fears;

Fill me with Thy power
To carry out Thy will;

Fill me with Thy wisdom
To teach the listening ear

Help me to wait patiently
As You guide me through each day;

Leading me and teaching me,
As You change my sinful ways.

Work in me Thy Fathers will
As I yield my owns to You;

Take my life, my heart, my all
And do as You so choose

I Am Willing

With a humble heart
And on bending knees
I came to Jesus
And asked Him please,

"If You are willing, LORD,
You can make me clean."

You can cleanse me from
The stench of sin;
You can cleanse me from
The shame within;

You can free me from
My past hurts;
You can deliver me from
All generational curses;

You can change my cross
Into a crown;
You can unlock the chains
That has me bound;

You can wash me in
Your redeeming blood;
You can keep me in
Your precious love:

If You're willing LORD,
You can liberate me,
You can save me unto eternity.

He stretched out His hand
Touching me saying,

"I AM willing, be clean."
I'm willing, just believe"!

I've set you free from the stench of sin;
I've set you free from shame within;

I'm freeing you from past hurts;
I'm freeing you from
All generational curses;

I've changed your cross into a crown;
I've unlocked the chains that
Had you bound;

I've washed you in My redeeming blood;
I'm keeping you in My precious love.

I AM willing.
I'VE SET YOU FREE
I'VE SAVED you unto ETERNITY

Just Say The Word

Just say the word LORD and the lame shall walk;
Just say the word and the mute will talk.

Just say the word LORD and the deaf shall hear;
Just say the word and my storms will clear.

Just say the word LORD and the blind shall see
Just say the word and I will be set free.

"Such great faith I have not seen.
So be it unto to you as you believe."

Just say the word LORD and darkness shall flee;
Just say the word and my torment will cease.

Just say the word LORD and shackles will fall off;
Just say the word and I'll no longer be lost.

Just say the word LORD and my child will be healed
Just say the WORD and PEACE will be still.

"Such great faith I have not seen.
So be it unto you as you believe."

Thy Staff

Stretch out Thy staff and search me,
Lay bear the secrets of my heart,
Uncover my most hidden parts

Let Thy staff be a light
To guide me through
My darkest night:

Through valleys shadowed
By death along the road;
A journey only to You is known.

Through hell's storms,
Through fiery darts
Aimed at my mind
And my heart

Pass my worried and
Through my doubts
To the place where my
Sins are rooted out

Where pride dies
And will is sustained;
Where sin and shame
Can stake no claim

Take me to my
Desert place,
Where trials and testing
Shape my faith

That place of "True Repentance"
Where I seek your face:
Where I pray and I wait, and I wait . . .

Until the power Of Your Spirit
Transforms me
Into the image of Your Son;

Until the light Of Your Word
Birth in me
The Fruit of Your love,

Until living water
Breaks forth
Like mountain springs.

Until my heart rejoice
And begin to sing

Of higher ground;
That place in You

Where I'm
No longer bound:

Where I walk
In the liberty of
Christ's shed blood,

Where I share freely
Your unconditional love,

And feast on the wonders
Of all You've done.

He Restores My Soul

Caught in the snares
Of my wandering ways,

Defeated under the weight
Of evil's sway:

Cast down by sin,
Despair waging war within:

Struggling to set myself free,
From sins that so easily beset me;

From self deceit and
Hidden pride and

From the one
Who wishes my demise?

I pray, I wait, I wail,
Seem to no avail . . .

O' but the moment
You heard my cry,

You left the ninety-nine
And hurried to my side

You freed me from my burdens,
You carried my heavy load;

You stood me on my feet
As You sought to make me whole

You refreshed me with Your presence
Assured me of Your love;

Tenderly correcting me as
You restored my wounded soul

You changed my song of sorrow
To triumph and victory;

To praise and thanksgiving
For the One who sets me free

My Life Is Yours

Dear Father,
My life is Yours, to keep
Yours to enfold,
Each part Yours to control

You lead and I'll follow,
You call and I'll come;

Running to Your side as
You guide me by and by;

Through valley lows
And mountains highs,

Through desert plains
And rough terrain . . .

Through the darkest
Hours of the night,

Until the Son—shine
His brightest light

To pastures ever so green
To clear water streams,

To the land flowing
With milk and honey,

That place of rest
For my soul,
Where fear gives way
To sweet repose

I Belong To You

Dear Jesus, when I look
Into Your eyes,
I see a love so divine;

A love that knows me
Most intimately;
And still You love me
Unconditionally

My heart rejoice,
My soul delights
In the truth that
Sets my ways aright

Yes, I'm satisfied
Just knowing You
No, no other will ever do.

I belong to You,
You belong to me;

Like a shepherd
Who owns His sheep,
I'm Yours to keep.

My spirit leaps
Inside of me,
When I hear You calling me.

I jump for joy,
I run to You
Happy to see Your face;

All my fears
Washed away;
Now at Your feet I lay.

Contented to be
Your little sheep;
In Your care to keep:

I belong to You,
You belong to me;

Like a shepherd
Who owns His sheep,
I am Yours to keep.

Romans 8:1

There is therefore now no condemnation to those who are in Christ Jesus, who do not walk according to the flesh, but according to the Spirit

Bid Me To Come

Kiss me with
The kisses of Your mouth
Wash me with Your WORDS

Anoint me with oils
Frankincense, Aloe and Myrrh

Take me into Your chambers
Into the depths of Your love

Bid me to come
My darling my dove

And I will delight in You
I will worship my Beloved

I will delight in You
I shall rejoice in Your Love

When You bid me to come
My whole life will change

When You bid me to come
I won't be the same

I won't talk the same,
Walk the same, look the same,
I'll be changed

Like the birth of a butterfly
I'll have a new life

Change by the
Beauty of Your love

FREE to be Your
Faithful dove

Soaring high like
An eagle in flight

Glowing bright like
A star in the night

Bring glory to your name
My Redeemer
My Deliverer,
My God and
My King

Bid me to come
My darling my dove

And I will delight in You
I will worship my Beloved

I will delight in You
I will rejoice in Your Love

I Want To Know You Lord

I want to know You LORD.
I want to know that You're real
I want to hear Your heart beat
I want to know how You Feel

I want to smell the fragrance of
Your Presence where ever I go
I want to touch the hem of Your
Garment and be made whole

I want to see You
The moment I open my eyes
I want to know You as my Son-rise

I want to taste of Your goodness
And be a witness to everyone I meet,
In the assembly, in the streets

Change my heart LORD
No matter what it take;
Show me the way of obedience
And how to walk by faith

Let me know You Like
Abraham, Isaac and Jacob
LORD increase my faith,
Let me hear You when You say
Follow Me, this is the way

Let me know You like Adam
In the cool of the day
Meet with me LORD,
In Your secret place

Let me know You like Mary,
Whatever Thy will,
So be it unto me.

Let me know You my Jesus,
My Savior, my LORD.
Let me know You like Enoch
Who walked with God
And was no more

Let me know You like Moses:
In the parting of the sea
Use me LORD to help
Set your people free.

Let me know You like Esther
For such a time as this
To walk in my purpose
And fulfill my assignment

Let me know You like Job:
In my suffering, in my sorrows
Let me know You LORD
And Your resurrection power:

Let me know you like David:
A man after Your own heart.
From me Dear LORD
Let Your Spirit never depart.

I want to know You Father
And Your Only Begotten Son.
Not my will, LORD,
But Yours be done.

Heaven's Most Precious Treasure

I have no gold
No frankincense
Nor myrrh
To celebrate
My Savior's birth
A broken life
Is all I have
To offer unto Thee;
This wounded heart
Scared and dark
I lay humbly
At Your feet
Forgive me
My transgression
My iniquities, my sins,
Wash me, cleanse me
Make me whole again
All my tears,
My hidden fears,
I surrender
Unto You
Take my life,
My will, my all
And do as You
So choose
Work in me
Thy Father's will
To do of Thy
Good pleasure;
Birth in me the likeness
Of heaven's most
Precious treasure:

The Betrayal Of Thy Love

Forgive me, Dear Jesus,
For betraying Thee with a kiss;
I sought my own desires,
I was led by my flesh.
Forgive my selfish motives
And every prayer asked amiss.
I did not seek Your Kingdom
With all my heart and soul;
I did not place my life
In Your loving control:
I trusted my own wisdom
And didn't believe in You;
Although I called You LORD
I was not surrendered to You.
I betrayed my fellow Christians
With my wandering ways;
Causing some to stumble
As they traveled on their way:
Forgive me, Dear Jesus,
For my multitude of sins;
Take from me dishonor and
Make me whole again.
Wash me O' SAVIOR
In Thy precious blood;
Teach me to be FAITHFUL
To never spurn Thy love

Go deep within the chambers
The chambers of my heart;
Reveal to me the secrets
That keeps me in the dark.
Give me a REVELATION
Of what the cross is all about?
And help me to embrace suffering
And pour my life out.
Let not my life be wasted,
Nor let me be put to shame,
But let me be a witness
Who brings GLORY
To Your name
The one thing I desire,
The thing I want the most,
Is to really know You Father,
Son and Holy GHOST
So teach me Holy Spirit
What it really, really means,
To keep my FAITH in JESUS
And truly BELIEVE!!
Fill me with COMPASSION,
With Your MERCY and GRACE,
And let me be of SERVICE
To those who go astray.
Fill me with Your POWER
To teach and show the way
Of how to keep our focus
And not lose sight of You
And how to keep our FAITH,
Our HOPE, our TRUST
In ALL You say and do.

Change Me

Change me Dear Jesus,
Make me more like you
That I may glorify the Father too

Remove this O' wineskin,
Sinned brittle and torn
Heavy with doubt, weak and worn

Create in me a new heart,
That beats only for You
Fill it with love:
With mercy always new
Fill it with rejoicing
Praise and gratitude

Grant me Thy wisdom Lord
In all that I do
In every trial and tribulation
That I may count it all joy

Teach me to hold my peace
To let You fight my battles
And keep the enemy under my feet

So change me Lord,
Change me inside and out.
Take the coals and touch my lips
Sanctify every word that
Comes from my mouth;

My motives, my desires,
My thoughts, my dreams

My heart, my faith,
My hopes, my deeds;

From the top of my head
To the bottom of my feet,

LORD I'm asking You
To change me

Every time I come before You
Don't let me leave the same

Do whatever You must do
To make that eternal exchange

Change me Lord
So that I can be more like You
Change me Lord and
Get the glory You're so due.

The Master Gardenar

Like a budding rose
A creation so rare
You're in need of my special care

Radiant with glory delicate and fine
An elegant Master piece
By the Creator Divine

To you I pledged My love
That day My Son the Chosen One

Hung between to thieves
To seal our love unto eternity

Come to Me, I bid thee
Come learn from Me and I will teach you
How to walk in the ways of My love

Come and allow Me to till
The grounds of Your heart and pull out
The root cause of your fears

Let the water of My love
Wash away all of your ills

Sit with Me in the mist of the garden,
In that secret place of prayer
Bring me all of your cares;
I'll take all of your broken petals
And plant new seeds

I'll create new flowers
With new fragrances, new beauties
And new virtues

Come and discover the wonderful life
That I have prepared just for you
A life that can only be
Found in My presence,

That can only found in My Word,
That can only be found in an
Intimate relationship with Me
A life that's waiting just for you

Come, I bid thee. I'm waiting for you.
Come and trust the console of My Spirit

And allow Me to lead you into
An abundant life of Righteousness
Peace and Joy . . . .

Come taste and see that I am good.
Come take from the Tree of Life
Come drink the sweet nectars
Of My love and be full.

Your faith will increase
Each time we meet
And each time you obey Me
Your garden will overflows with my glory;

With kindness, wisdom and generosity,
With peace, patience and joy,
With mercy, humility and much more

Praise Me! Praise Me OFTEN!
Especially when times are hard,
For each time you do,
You will experience sweet victory!

I LOVE YOUR PRAISE!
Your praise is like
A bouquet of freshly cut roses

And like an alabaster jar
Broken and poured
The fragrance of your praise fills
My throne room with joy

I bid thee, Come
That I may bless you
I want to give you gifts
To bless other with

Messages of hope and
Faith for the weary,
Compassion to comfort the heart
A healing balm for
The broken and wounded

I Am
The Master Gardener

I want you to trust Me with your heart,
Trust every seed that I plant in you

Even the ones you don't understand
For they are all meant for your good

And will soon
Bring about your Orchids;
Your Mature Charm; The Glory of My Son

So that you may be a light
To help guide the lost,

To the foot of the cross

Come I bid thee,
COME!

Patch Work

Broken hearts repaired,
Sewn together
By those who care

Heart of God displayed,
By the things you do and say.

You receive truth from
The Father,
To help lighten the load
Of weary soul:

Your time, your prayers,
Your servant heart,
A light to lead us out of the dark:

Where shattered lives
Are weakened by sin,

You pour love in
To heal and mend

Imparting knowledge,
Strength,
Hope and faith
Compassion, assurance forgiveness
God's glorious grace:

As you serve
The Father above
Our hearts are knitted
Together for eternity in love

Whispers In The Night

Hush thy worries!
Silent thy fears
Wipe away thy tears
Listen! Take heed! Hear!

When the way seems
To be unclear
Come to me,
Draw near for
I AM waiting,
I AM here
To guide the
Listening ear
No need to fret,
No need to doubt
I AM the alter
For all thy fears
I AM the cloud
That led by day and
I AM the fire
That led by night
I AM the whisper
In the night seasons
That leads you to the light.

Hush thy worries!
Silent thy fears
Wipe away thy tears!
Listen! Take heed! Hear!

Intimacy

In to me You see LORD,
Into my heart where the truth be told
Where pain and sorrow has shattered my soul

Where sin, shame lay claim
To hidden secrets only You know.

In to me You see LORD,
Into my inter-most being where
Affliction and misery tries to imprison me

And where darkness tries to take control
It is here where my motives are exposed
And where Your illuminating eyes
Divides the truth from the lies.

Here in the battle field of my mind
Where life and death are fought
Is where Your WORD takes
Captive every deceiving thought.

It is here where Your Spirit whispers to me
"Come my child, you have been set free,
Trust and believe in My Only Son
Trust that Calvary's work is done."

Here in the
Chambers of my heart,
Is where I receive Your mercy
And accept Your grace
It is here as Your child
I take my place.

It is here where
Your word affirms me,
And Your power fills me,
Where I'm healed by Your stripes
And guided by Your light.

Here in the sanctuary of my heart,
Where Your Spirit abides,
Is where Your blood covers me
And where You love me
Unconditionally.

I Can't Wait

I can't wait to look into His eyes
And know that I'm his bride
To hear him call my name
To know the glory of the One
Who took away my shame

I can't wait to hold his hands
And touch the place where the nails went in
To free me from an eternal curse,
And from words that damage and hurt

I can't wait to kiss His face
In the very place that was struck and marred
To remove from me all
Accusations laid to my charge

I can't wait to hold Him close in my arms
And feel the back that was beaten and torn
To win for me all victories
From illness, pain and all disease

I can't wait to touch the place
Where He was pierced
Where blood and tears gushed
To heal my heart that
Was broken and crushed

Or to kiss His blessed feet that
Was nailed to the cross
To save my soul
So that I wouldn't be lost

The very feet that
To pave the way for me to be free
Oppression and poverty

I can't wait
To whisper in His ears
And tell Him how I feel

To say thank You JESUS,
My God and my King,
Thank You Lord, for everything

It's Finished

It's finished, it's finished
The victory is already won
He broke the curse at Calvary
And won for me ALL victories
Through His blood He shed for me

Now guiltless I stand before the King
Declaring what He's done for me

I'm free, I'm free
Free to love and live again
Free to forgive my fellow man
Free from every disease known to man
From heart break, sickness and pain
Free from oppression, poverty and ruin
Free to share what Jesus has done
Free to hope in what's to come

I'm free, I'm free
To walk by faith and not by sight
To be led by the Spirit and follow Christ

Meet Me In My Dream Jesus

Meet me in my dream Jesus
Meet me in my dream
When I lay me down to sleep
Come let me know You're near
Come share the wonders of Your love
Come hold me close and dear
Come let the fire of Your Spirit
Burn away my fears.

Meet me in my dream Jesus
Meet me in my dream
Where I celebrate Your Presence
And gaze upon your face
Where I dance and rejoice
In Your glory and Your grace.

Meet me in my dream Jesus
Meet me in my dream
Come ease my weary soul
Come let me hear you say
I'll never leave or forsake you
I'm with you always
Come share with me the secret
The secret of your heart
That I am child of the light
And not of the dark.

Forgive Me Dear Father

Forgive me, Dear Father,
For the things
I've said and done;

I've fallen by the way
And betrayed Thy Holy One

Grant me Thy great favor,
Wash me with Thy blood;

Forgive me my Betrayal,
The spurning of Thy love:

Lift me with Thy power,
From the valley below;

Lead me into high country,
Where living waters flow:

Restore to me Thy Spirit,
Thy mercy and Thy grace;

Keep me in Thy presence,
Turn away not Thy face.

Work in me Thy pleasure,
That Thy will be done;

Make me a reflection,
Of Thy loving Son:

Romans 4:7-8

"Blessed is the one whose iniquities are forgiven and whose sins have been completely eradicated. And blessed is the one whose sin the Lord will not take account of."

Eternal Love

I heard my Father calling,
Beckoning me to come,
Listen to the story
Of His eternal love

Dear child He said to me
"There's something you should know.
Remember what I tell you, and never let it go."

My love for you is eternal. My love will never end.
I'll always be Your Father, Your Savior and Your friend.

There's nothing in this world that can take My love from you. All you
have to do is believe this is true.

Before I created the heavens, before I created the Earth, My love for you
came first.

Before I called on light to separate day from night,
You were the apple of My eye who never left My sight.

Before rivers, lakes and streams gathered into the Seas, before dry land
appeared and mountains peaked;

Before plants and trees came to be,
Before they were able to yield seeds;
Before time told the seasons when to start,
You were the love of my heart.

Before I scattered the stars in space
And sat each planet in its place;
Before oceans teamed with life
Or a single bird took flight;

Before lilies, roses and daffodils,
Before any beast ever roamed the fields,
I loved you.

Before the world begun,
Before I hung the moon or made the sun;

I chose My Only begotten One
To shed His precious blood,
To prove to you My love."

From eternity to eternity
As far as east is from west,
My love for you will always exist.

Before man's fall, I made a call
And you were on the list.

Yes, I foreknew you,
Familiar with all your ways,
Knew everything about you,
What you'd do and what you'd say;
And still my love remains the same.

You're My GREATEST CREATION.
I created you with all my love:
I made you in My image
To reflect the glory of My Son:

Now hear My Beloved.
And listen with your heart.

I'll never leave or forsake you
We'll never be apart

Now this is My promise,
My Word unto you;

Believe Me when I tell You
And receive it when I say,

I loved you THEN
I love you NOW
I'll love you ALWAYS.

Love Is

Love, is not just a word,
It's a way of being;
It's a verb.

Love is always doing,
Always giving,
It always serves.

Love seeks out
The needs of others
And is eager to please;

It builds others up,
In word and indeed:

Love poured out on its
Desired affection,
Breaks the chains of
Selfishness, hate and shame:

Selfless in its motive,
Love's only aim
Is to set others free
So that they too
Can love, unconditionally!

The Color Of Love

The color of love
Is a dove descending from above
The color of love
Is remembering to give a hug

The color of love
Is sunflower awaking to
A brand new day:
The color of love
Is a smile on a child's face:

The color of love
Is a family sharing evening meals
The color of love
Is a praying mother as she kneels:

The color of love
Is the tear in the eyes of a bride
The color of love
Is the sound of a newborn baby's cry.

The color of love . . .
Is fall leaves blowing in the breeze.
The color of love . . .
Is the taste of summer ice cream.

The color of love . . .
Is spring bringing forth new life.
The color of love . . .
Is the celebration between
A husband and his wife:

The color of love
Is putting others first.
The color of love
Is giving a cool glass of water
To quench a thirst:

The color of love . . .
Is a rainbow in the sky
The color of love . . .
Is a caterpillar turned butterfly.

The color of love . . .
Is the beauty of the sunset as the day ends.
The color of love . . .
Is the whispering of the wind.

The color of love . . .
Is learning how to be a friend:
The color of love . . .
Is forgiving again and again:

The color of love . . .
Is an eagle soaring high.
The color of love . . .
Is the dance of the dragonfly.

The color of love . . .
Is saying "I'm sorry" and
Really meaning it
The color of love . . .
Is the freedom to receive it.

The color of love is dining by candlelight.
The color of love . . .
Is being serenaded at night:

The color of love . . .
Is to share Jesus with the lost:
The color of love . . .
Is to help carry someone else's cross:

The color of love . . .
Is God's chosen sacrifice:
The color of love . . .
Is Jesus laying down His life:

The color of love . . .
Is His favor and His grace:
The color of love . . .
Is that He took my place.

The color of love . . .
Is the returning of the Son.
The color of love . . .
Is surrendering my will
That His be done.

A Love Letter

He gave me a letter
Each page was filled with love
He wrote it with a pen
Filled with Emanuel's blood
He sent it from heaven
On the wings of a dove

He laid it in a manger
For all the world to see
Then He sent his holy angels
To serenade the king

They sung of His GLORY
They sung with great joy
They offered good tiding
Of hope, peace and love

I picked up His letter
And held it close to me
I read every line
And pondered its mysteries

I read every word
With caution and care
They melted my heart
And took away my fears

He said He'll always love me
That he'd never leave me alone
Said he would laid down His very life
To make me His own
Said he would go to the cross
To right every wrong

He told me not to worry
To always trust and believe
That no matter what happens
He would return for me

To trust Him in the valley
Through rain and the storms
To praise Him through the night
And He'll be my Peace and my calm

He said that every single trail
Is just a grow my faith
To build me up and make me strong
So that I can walk in His ways

Said to never let my struggles
Take my joy away
But to praise Him through it all
Until the break of day

Amazing Grace

Amazing grace,

Amazing grace

O' how can this be

Amazing grace, amazing grace

His love covers me

A sinner made guiltless

Forgiven set free

By the blood of the Lamb

That was shed for me

Protected by mercy

Kept by grace

Surrounded by favor

O' what a wonderful day

What a wonderful place

What blessed assurance

His amazing love

His amazing grace

2 Corinthians 12:9

And He said to me, "My grace is sufficient for you, for My strength is made perfect in weakness . . ."

Celebrate!

When we celebrate . . .
We invite the King of
Glory to come in
We make a joyful
Noise to our King!

We laugh, we cry,
We sing, we dance,
We stomp our feet
And clap our hands!

We say,
"Yes and Amen;
Thy Will be done."
For You are the
RIGHTEOUS and HOLY ONE."

When praises go up,
Blessings come down;
Salvation, forgiveness;
Peace and joy
For in His presence
Abundant life is found!

Like morning dew
He falls on us
Fulfilling our thirst,
To be made new

He receive our adoration,
Our worship, our praise,
He hears our petition,
Our repentance and
How I bless His name.

His Spirit Work:
Death and rebirth
To transform and conform
Our image to His

As our heart lay bare
He tenderly purges
Us from our worldly cares

Chains are loosed and
Shackles fall off
When we stand in submission
At the foot of the cross

When we celebrate
We invite the King of
Glory to come in
We make a joyful
Noise to our King

We say "Yes and Amen;
Thy will be done
For You are the
RIGHTEOUS and HOLY ONE"

Heaven Is

It's the transformation of my soul
It's the washing of the WORD that makes me whole

It's peace in the midst of a ragging storm
It's the gift of a child being born

It's faith that sees beyond my darkest nights
Truth that breaks forth like Son—light

It's the gathering of the harvest from the fields
It's breaking bread and sharing a meal

It's the fire of God that's shut up in my bones
It's planting seeds as I pen this poem

It's spreading the Gospel and winning the lost
It's helping a sista' carry her cross

It's looking down on that brotha' just to lift him up
It's the practice of love and forgiveness

It's meeting new people and making new friends
It's pursuing peace with all men

It's what I say and the things I do
To bring life, healings and blessing to you

It's the freedom to choose love over hate
It's the presence of God that leads the way

It's holding my peace and letting him fight
It's laying down pride and walking in the light

It's overcoming by the blood of the lamb
It's understanding, who I am

A child of Gods a princess and a Queen
It's representing the city of "New Jerusalem"

It's making disciples and loving souls
It's taking back what the enemy stole

It's knowing "Jesus" yes the "Father and the "Son"
It's declaring Gods Kingdom that His Will Be Done

It's Jesus hanging between two thieves
Shedding His blood for you and me

It's RESURRECTION, the revealing of the Son
Its Jews and Gentiles united as one

Casting crowns at His feet
It's being content just to be His sheep

It's the Glory of God that makes my heart rejoice
It's all of creation with lifted voice

Worshipping the Lamb that was slain
It's life eternal with the Kings of kings

You Got To Know Jesus

You got to Know Jesus,
You got to know Christ
You got to know Jesus
If you want to raise me right

We're made in His image,
Reflecting His light
You got to know Jesus
He's the answer to our life

You're chosen, handpicked,
To be my Pop
My teacher, my provider,
My protector, my rock

My leader, my friend,
My example, my guide
I'm a blank piece of paper
And you're writing my life

Everything you say and
Everything you do
You better be careful
Because I'm looking at you

My cool, my swag,
My personality
It's all a combination
Of what you put in me

If you respect the ladies,
I'll respect them too
But if you play 'em and you hate 'em
What you think I'm going to do?

If you're ganging and slanging
If you're in and out of jail
If you ROCK IT like that
Then my life will be HELL

If you shoot it and you toot it
If you pop it and you drop it
I'm asking you to stop it
Cause that aint how you "Rock It"

All I'm trying to say is
You got to have a plan
Cause you can raise a boy
Or you can raise a man

I'm asking you to do your best
To raise this kid with self respect

Now look in the mirror
Tell me what to you see
When you look in the mirror
Know you're looking at me

So change the man in the mirror
To make it better for me
Because when I grow up I want to be like you
Cause you're my number one hero
You're my number one cool

That's why you got to know Jesus
You got to know Christ
You got to know Jesus
If you want to raise me right

We're made in His image
Reflecting His light
You got to know Jesus
He's the answer to our life

Who Is This

Who is this that
Spoke to the wind and it obeyed?
Who is this that
Kings worshipped as a Babe?

Who is this that
Can make blind men see?
Who is this that
Causes demons to tremble and flee?

Who is this that
Came to set the captive free?
Who is this that I hear calling me?

His name is Jesus,
Emmanuel,
God with us;
The Holy One of Israel,
Our Messiah

Son of God, Son of man
The Lion and the Lamb
He's Deity In humanity
Who came to save us

Who is this that
Heals the sick and raises the dead?
Who is this that
Fed five thousand with two fish
And some bread?

Who is this that
Causes leaves clap their hands?
Who is this that
Forgives the sins of man?

Who is this that
Holds the key to hell,
Death and the grave?

Who is this that
Was crucified so that I
Would be saved?

His name is Jesus,
Emmanuel,
God with us;
The Holy One of Israel,
Our Messiah

Son of God, Son of man
The Lion and the Lamb
He's Deity In humanity
Who came to save us

Let's Go Into The Father's House

Let's go into the Father's house
To celebrate the King;
Let's go into the Father's house
To magnify His name:

He does signs and wonders
In heaven and earth
He does signs and wonders
In heaven and earth

Merciful and Gracious
Is the King of kings;
Merciful and Gracious
His love will always reign.

Forgiving transgression, iniquities and sins
Forgiving generations again and again

Revealing heaven's secrets
To His faithful ones;
Revealing heaven's secrets
The glory of His Son:

Powerful and Mighty
Are You O' LORD
Powerful and Mighty
To You we lift our voice.

You show signs and wonders
In the heavens and on earth
You show sighs and wonders
In the heaven and on earth

The Only True Power

The only true power
For those who are lost,
The only true power
Is the power of the cross.

Give your life to Jesus
Lay it down today,
Give your life to Jesus
He'll wash your sins away.

Mercy and forgiveness
Is His gift to you,
Mercy and forgiveness
Is what He has for you

Can't you hear Him calling,
Calling out your name:
Can't you hear Him calling
Now let the Savior in.

He's knocking at the door
The door of your heart
He's knocking at the door
To give you a brand new start.

Open up the door
And let His love come in
Open up the door
And He'll forgive you of your sins!

"Treasure I Found"

He's my diamond in a coal mind
He's my pearl in the sea
He's everything I want
And everything I need

He's this girl's best friend
Through thick and thin
He's the reason why
I'm living once again

He's the sparkle in my eyes
And the smile on my face
He's the reason why
I love Him more everyday

He's the song in my heart
And the joy in my soul
He's the reason why I sing
I want everyone to know

He's the "Treasure I found
Hidden in a field
He's not a fake or a con
He's the real deal

I'll give Him my heart,
My soul and my will
I'll sell all I have
Just to be with him

Cause He took me from my darkness
And he brought me to His light

Forgave of my sins
And made my heart right

He swept me off my feet
And He made me whole

He's the lover of my soul
Who refines me like gold

He took all my sorrows,
Because I gave Him my pain

He took all my weakness,
And He freed me from my shame

I have nothing to lose,
I've got everything to gain

Since He called me to the cross
To make that "Great Exchange"

Resurrection

It was on a dark and dreary cloud filled day
When all our sins were washed away

When the Savior hung between earth and sky
Beaten, bloody: crucified

He paid a debt we could not pay
He died a death we should have died

The hounds of hell were hissing loud
Laughing, mocking hurling chides

Legions furry Satan's last try
To end the Saviors precious life

Heavens tears fell from on high
Lighting flashing striking pride
Piercing darkness exposing lies

Thunder trumpet God's heart cry
My Beloved Son, I CRUCIFIED
To save the guilty;
Innocence must die

Ground shaking, trembling quaking
Descending to the world beneath
He led captivity captive
He set the sinner free

He conquered hell, death and the grave
He took the keys and He crushed that Snake
And won for thee all victories
Through His blood He shed for thee

Then early morning that third day
When the Angles rolled that stone away
Jesus rose up and walked away

His glory shown in brilliant ways (rays)
Cause death couldn't hold Him in that grave

Now every day I celebrate
"Jesus is alive"
"Jesus is alive

"Oh grave where is your victory is?
'Oh death where is your sting?

"Jesus has risen from the dead,
He's risen just like He said

Jesus has risen from the dead
He is the "Risen King"

God Saved Me!

He saved me. God saved me.
He called me out from a life
That was hell bound
Where boundaries had no limits
And freedom didn't exist.

A selfish life, lead by the flesh;
A rebellious life that gave
Birth to foolishness;

He offered me eternal life,
Abundant life through His sacrifice,
That day He hung on Calvary's tree
And took the place that was meant for me;

He forgave me of all my sins,
Never to remember them again;
He washed me in His redeeming blood,
And covered me with unconditional love;

He sealed me with His Holy Spirit
To be presented before Him
Without spot or blemish;

He made me one with the
Father, the Spirit and the Son;

He set me apart and
Gave me a brand new start,
With a brand new heart;

Filled me with treasures from above,
His power, His compassion,
His mercy, His love;

He gave me the ability to believe,
To walk by faith and not by sight
To trust the plan He has for my life.

He's now changing me, sanctifying me,
Restoring my soul and making me whole.

Setting me free from secret sins
Hidden in chambers deep within.

He uses all my trials, tribulations
Circumstances and situation

To rescue me from myself, my fears,
The opinion of my peers,

And from the one who wishes my demise
That ole serpent, the "father of lies"

He's teaching me obedience, to obey His will;
To praise Him through it all,
No matter what I think or feel.

And how to love Him with all of myself
While He teaches me to love everyone else;

And how to worship Him in spirit and truth,
To bring glory to His name
By letting my words and my deeds be the same.

That I might be a testimony of His love,
A living witness of How
God **O**wn **S**on **P**urchased **E**ternal **L**ife

For you and me
So that we can be free

The Call

There's a call
In the stillness of your heart,
A call to be set apart;

To fellowship with the Father,
To be one among
Many sons and daughters

A call to freedom,
From sin and shame
From darkness to light,

To live a victorious, abundant life
A call to walk by faith and not by sight
To a surrendered obedient life;

To bring honor to the Son
To let His will be done
To be covered in His righteousness,

Adorned with His holiness
A worshipper who worships
In spirit and in truth

So that the power of the blood
May be revealed in you

There's a call, can't you hear it?
To be one with the
Father, Son and Holy Spirit

A call to trumpet the alarm
To preach the GOSPEL
That God's children will come

To be robed in white linen and
Presented before Him
Without spot or blemish;

To be His bride awaiting
Her soon coming groom

To be arrayed in
A garment of praise
That we may bless the

Father above thanking Him
For His love

I Met A Friend

I met a friend
A delightful, gentle, pleasant man
Respectful, courteous and kind

I met a friend
A humble soul,
Full of wisdom, full of light

We sat, we ate, and we talked
He inquired about my life

He was curious, curious to know,
"What moved my soul"?

What treasures had I
Discovered along the road?

What concluding answers
To life mysteries did I find?

What encounter as I
Traveled renewed my mind?
I sensed him searching
For his own answers
I sensed him searching for "The Light"

For through his many questions,
I began to understand
That the Lover of my soul,
Was pursuing this precious man

Oh' Heavens joy, Oh' how it lifted me
To see the mercy of the my LORD
Calling out to He

As we looked into
The windows of our lives

Back to memories past
And to what the futures wholes

I spoke the only truth I know

I pointed to the cross
For all our victories won

I point to our hearts
For those yet to come

Then the time we shared
Came to an end
And I found myself full and satisfied

Not from the food we ate
But from the company of the "friend" I just met

I met a friend
I met someone I know,
I'll see again

Have You Cried Today

Have you cried today?
Have you cried for the lost?

Have you lent a hand
To help carry a cross?

Have you walked in
Your brotha' shoes?

Do you know what
Your sista' been through?

Do you feel his pain?
Do you know her sorrow?

Do you care if they
Have hope for tomorrow?

Will you show them some mercy?
Will you give them some grace?

Will you share your strength?
Will you share your faith?

Will you break some bread
With a hungry soul?

Will you invite them in
From out of the cold?

Will you clothe the naked
With you prayers?

Will you lift them up
To receive the Fathers care?

Will you lead them to the Rock
Who can fill their thirst?

Will you tell them about Jesus
And why He came to earth?

Show them that He loves them,
That He cares for the lost.

Be a friend and help carry a cross.

You Are Not Alone

You're not alone;
Waves of love now flood
Louisiana, Mississippi
And the Alabama plains

To help those who were
Laid waste by Katrina's Hurricane

You're not alone;
We stand with you
Through this catastrophe
We feel your sorrow;

We share your grief,
We are here to bring you relief

You're not alone;
You're in our prayers and in our hearts
Let us help make you a brand new start

Let us lift your spirits and
Help rebuild your lives
With our compassion, our resource,
Our efforts, our time,

Let the light of God's love
And the power of His might
Lead you out of your darkest night

You're not alone;
Hold on to hope, don't let her go

Let her pave the way to better days
Let her dream of new beginnings
Let her dance the dance of triumph
Let her sing songs of victory
Let her shout out to those

Who gaze in wonder? "We're not defeated,
"We're not alone"

Let each heart beat for every child found
Who was torn from its mother's arms

Let each thought be for those who
Made it through the storm

Let each tear be for those
Who are forever lost

Let each desire be to help
Carry one another's cross

Let hope live and not die.
For you have survived

You're not alone
We stand at your side

The Day The Earth Shook Haiti

Surrounded by concrete and dirt
An infant cries out from
Deep within the earth

A mother hears. No time for worry
No time to doubt. No time for fear.

Now standing at Thy mercy seat
Deep cries out to deep.

Oh heaven give ear.

She digs and shovels and scoops,
Refusing to quit, refusing to stop,

Throwing back rubble, tossing back rocks
Refusing to be deterred by aftershocks;

Lifting boulders with the help
Of many shoulders

She pushes and strains her
Way through hours of labor

Toiling, sweating,
Working to free her child

From the belly of the lifeless
Womb that now held it bound.

She forges on driven by faith,
Driven by hope, driven by love . . .

Until mercy is released from above

Until heaven commands
The earth to give birth

Until her little one is once again
Cradled in the safety of her arms

And hears her heart beat and
Feels the comfort of her warmth

"Oh sweet victory, Praise the God
Who hears and sees!"

Shouts of joy and tears
Collides at the site of this rescue

Heaven and earth
Both rejoice for the soul that
Lives on to one day tell the story

Of how faith and mercy met
How God stretch out His hand
And lifted him from the land

A Love That Never Dies

Orphaned children souls they cry
To have someone stand by their side

Possessing virtues noble and wise
That humbles spirit which heaven guide

With a strong and sturdy head held high
Boldly protecting a mothers prize

Who'll teach them how to live their life
Who'll raise them in the way that right

For welcome arms open wide
That warm embrace to cuddle and hide

A soft shoulder on which to cry
An angel's voice singing lullabies

For adoring eyes full of pride
For hands to tuck them in at night

And faithful knees praying on high
To guard and keep them from all lies

That sunlit mile that melts all fears
For attentive, patient listening ears

For gentle fingers wiping tears
To be that friend that's always near

Who'll celebrate them every year
That birthing day that brought them here

With joyful laughter trumpet loud
Just having fun with their child

Orphan children hear their cries
To never again be empty inside

For hearts that bleed just like Christ
That over flows into their lives

To fills their cups with
A love that never dies

2 Corinthians 3:16-18

" . . . but whenever a person turns to the Lord, the veil is taken away. Now the Lord is Spirit and where the Spirit of the Lord is there is, there is liberty. But we all, with unveiled face, beholding as in a mirror the glory of the Lord, are being transformed into the same image from glory to glory, just as from the Lord, the Spirit

Printed in the United States
By Bookmasters